INSIDE SPECIAL FORCES ™

SPECIAL OPS:
SEARCH AND RESCUE OPERATIONS

Carol Hand

rosen publishing's
rosen central

New York

Published in 2015 by The Rosen Publishing Group, Inc.
29 East 21st Street, New York, NY 10010

Copyright © 2015 by The Rosen Publishing Group, Inc.

First Edition

Library of Congress Cataloging-in-Publication Data

Hand, Carol, 1945–
Special ops: search and rescue operations/Carol Hand.
        pages cm.—(Inside Special Forces)
Includes bibliographical references and index.
ISBN 978-1-4777-7997-2 (library bound)—ISBN 978-1-4777-7998-9 (pbk.)—
ISBN 978-1-4777-7999-6 (6-pack)
1. Parachute troops—United States—Juvenile literature. 2. United States—Armed
Forces—Search and rescue operations—Juvenile literature. 3. United States. Air
Force—Search and rescue operations—Juvenile literature. 4. Special operations (Military
science)—Juvenile literature. 5. Special forces (Military science)—United States—Juvenile
literature. I. Title.
UD483.H37 2014
355.4—dc23

2014014620

Manufactured in Malaysia

CONTENTS

INTRODUCTION

The battle began as Operation Anaconda. U.S. troops were trying to overcome Al Qaeda and Taliban forces holed up in caves along the southern end of Afghanistan's Shah-e-Kot Valley. At 3:00 AM on March 4, 2002, a Chinook helicopter carrying U.S. Navy SEALs tried to land on Takur Ghar Mountain above the battlefield. But enemy forces bombarded the helicopter with machine-gun and rocket-propelled fire. As the crippled helicopter jerked upward, one SEAL, Petty Officer 1st Class Neil Roberts, was thrown out. The rest of the SEAL team escaped but quickly returned on a second Chinook to search for Roberts. A quick reaction force was also dispatched. This force included Army Rangers and two air force combat pararescue jumpers (PJs). One of the PJs was Senior Airman Jason Cunningham, twenty-six, assigned to the 38th Rescue Squadron, Moody Air Force Base, Georgia.

As the quick reaction force approached, two men, including Roberts, were already dead. The remaining SEALs were fighting for their lives. Enemy fire struck the helicopter while it was still 80 feet (24 meters) above the ground, and the now-wounded pilots managed to crash-land it. Rangers, PJs, and medics slid out the back and ran for cover.

The quick reaction force included five medical personnel, including Cunningham. They set up

Members of a Navy SEAL team exit an army CH-47D Chinook helicopter during training exercises. This type of helicopter delivered the quick reaction force during Operation Anaconda.

an emergency treatment facility in the Chinook's cargo hold on the bitterly cold mountain, surrounded by enemy fire. Soon they were treating ten seriously wounded soldiers. The enemy continued to bombard the helicopter. Then, the forward compartment caught fire. After four hours, Cunningham decided the cargo hold was too dangerous. Using a small sled, he made seven trips through enemy fire, moving the wounded to a second and then a third position. He and Sgt. Cory Lamoreaux, an army medic from the 160th Special Operations Aviation Regiment, grabbed weapons and fought off enemy fire to protect their patients. On the third move, Lamoreaux was shot in the abdomen. His wound was painful but not fatal. Then, at 12:32 PM, Cunningham was shot through the back, shattering his liver and causing severe internal bleeding.

Cunningham refused to believe he was badly injured. Although slowly bleeding out, he spent several more hours caring for patients, some with wounds less severe than his. He used one of two available blood packs to save a wounded Ranger. Medics gave the other to Cunningham himself, but he continued to lose blood. As his life faded, he gave instructions to others on how to care for the critically wounded. No rescue helicopter would be sent in to fly out the wounded until after dark. His fellow medical personnel tried hard to keep Cunningham alive, but he died at 6:00 PM. The medevac chopper arrived ninety minutes later.

Seven men, including Cunningham, died in the fight that became known as the Battle of Roberts' Ridge. Cunningham had been a PJ for only eight months, and this was his first field mission. His colleagues credited Cunningham with saving ten men that day. Six months after his death, Jason Cunningham was awarded the Air Force Cross, an award second only to the Medal of Honor. According to a fellow PJ, "Jason was right where every PJ wants to be. He was where guys needed him, and he was saving lives."

"THAT OTHERS MAY LIVE"

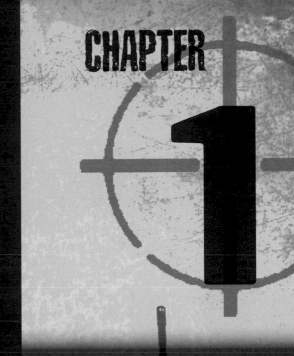

CHAPTER 1

Who are men like Jason Cunningham, who brave enemy fire and work under the harshest conditions to save those in danger? They are pararescue jumpers, or PJs, a highly trained, elite section of the military's Special Operations Forces. These fearless men can survive in extreme conditions. They track and locate people on land or at sea. They parachute in, use their medical training to stabilize wounded individuals, and extract them to safety. They do this even under enemy fire, and they return fire when necessary.

Pararescue jumpers (also called pararescuemen) are enlisted members of the U.S. Air Force. They comprise a small group of only three hundred to five hundred men, whose job is combat search and rescue, or CSAR (pronounced "C-sar"). Their motto sums up the goal and the importance of their job description: "These things we do, that others may live." Every

Pararescue jumpers, or PJs, parachute into rescue sites loaded with up to 170 pounds (77 kilograms) of gear. Here, a U.S. airman with the 306th Rescue Squadron carries out a training jump.

CSAR member must be willing to give his life to save others. SEALs, Army Rangers, and other Special Forces fighting units are considered the toughest of the tough in the armed forces. But when SEALs and Rangers are in trouble, they call on PJs for help.

WHERE PJS FIT

The Department of Defense considers rescue of its own so vital that it created an elite force, the Guardian Angel Weapon System (GAWS), specifically for CSAR missions. Normally, the term "weapon system" refers only to fighting hardware, such as jet aircraft. William F. Sine, a retired PJ, considers it a "singular honor" that the human component of this group is defined as part of a high-priority weapon system. The Guardian Angel Weapon System contains three human groups: pararescue jumpers, or PJs; combat rescue officers, or CROs (called "crows"); and SERE specialists (experts in survival, evasion, resistance, and escape).

GAWS is one of nine elite groups of Special Operations Forces (SOF) under the direction of the United States Special Operations Command (USSOCOM). These teams carry out special operations related to the war on terrorism. They seek out and destroy terrorist networks that threaten U.S. citizens and interests anywhere in the world. SOF teams are called the "Quiet Professionals." They are little known and do not seek publicity. This is partly because many of their missions are secret, and publicity would threaten their safety. But, in addition, most of these highly dedicated professionals just don't want the distraction of publicity. According to Baseops.net, SOFs, including PJs, live by four "truths":

1. Humans are more important than Hardware.
2. Quality is better than Quantity.
3. Special Operations Forces cannot be mass produced.
4. Competent Special Operations Forces cannot be created after emergencies occur.

SPECIAL OPERATIONS FORCES

CSAR personnel comprise one of nine elite Special Operations Forces. These are:

- Direct action: Raid and assault hostile targets

- Special reconnaissance (SR): Collect intelligence on targets

- Unconventional warfare (UW): Work with local forces in hostile or sensitive areas, using subversion, sabotage, guerrilla warfare, and covert operations

- Foreign internal defense: Train, advise, and assist local forces

- Civil affairs (CA): Coordinate U.S. military and foreign civilian activities with government and civilian organizations

- Counterterrorism: Locate and stop terrorist activities abroad

- Humanitarian assistance: Carry out humanitarian and disaster relief activities around the world

- Theater search and rescue: Rescue personnel from enemy territory when conventional search and rescue cannot

- Collateral mission areas: Cooperate with other forces to conduct security and protective activities such as security assistance, peacekeeping, and personnel recovery

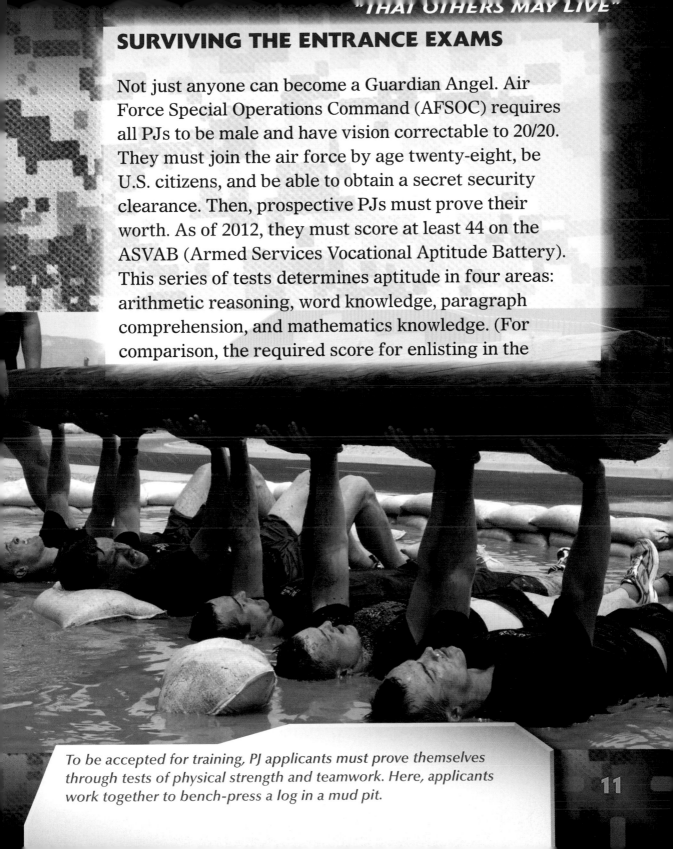

SURVIVING THE ENTRANCE EXAMS

Not just anyone can become a Guardian Angel. Air Force Special Operations Command (AFSOC) requires all PJs to be male and have vision correctable to 20/20. They must join the air force by age twenty-eight, be U.S. citizens, and be able to obtain a secret security clearance. Then, prospective PJs must prove their worth. As of 2012, they must score at least 44 on the ASVAB (Armed Services Vocational Aptitude Battery). This series of tests determines aptitude in four areas: arithmetic reasoning, word knowledge, paragraph comprehension, and mathematics knowledge. (For comparison, the required score for enlisting in the

To be accepted for training, PJ applicants must prove themselves through tests of physical strength and teamwork. Here, applicants work together to bench-press a log in a mud pit.

army or marines is 31; in the navy, 35; and in the air force, 36.) Next is the P.A.S.T. (Physical Ability and Stamina Test). This includes pull-ups, sit-ups, push-ups, and flutter kicks (all timed); a timed 3-mile (5 kilometer) run; two 25-meter (82 feet) underwater swims; and a 1,500-meter (5,000 feet) swim that must be completed in twenty-eight minutes. And that is just to get accepted for training.

SURVIVING PJ TRAINING

What follows is two full years of grueling training to make PJs who are the best of the best. Because the training is so intense, many PJs enter training after serving one or more tours as a soldier, sailor, airman, or marine. They continue physical training while going through the "PJ Pipeline." In this series of courses, they develop skills in weapons use, diving, parachuting, and survival in extreme environments. They also complete an emergency medicine (paramedic) course. They carry out mock training missions to practice putting all their skills together. During training, they develop expertise in all five stages of personnel recovery—report, locate, support, recover, and integrate.

Only one in ten trainees successfully completes PJ training. These few can call themselves pararescuemen. They are entitled to wear the signature maroon beret and the pararescue "angel" patch. But their training never ends. When not deployed, they constantly work to keep their skills sharp and take courses to keep up their paramedic certification.

WHAT PJS DO

Since the founding of pararescue in 1947, USAF pararescue personnel have served in all wars and have saved nearly forty thousand lives, according to retired PJ William Sine. Many of these were military lives, including downed pilots and other troops rescued during wartime. Some missions have been, and still are, top secret. In addition, PJs rescued all

A helicopter carrying PJs hovers over the Gemini-6 capsule, which splashed down in the Atlantic on December 16, 1965. In the background is the aircraft carrier USS Wasp.

Gemini astronauts during their ocean landings in the 1960s. They have assisted in large-scale humanitarian rescue operations, including those following the 1989 Loma Prieta earthquake, destruction of the twin towers in 2001, Hurricane Katrina in 2005, and Hurricane Sandy in 2012. PJs also rescue civilians, from injured mountain climbers to shipwrecked sailors.

Although PJs certainly have medical training, the military does not classify them as medics. Medics are noncombatants—they are not expected to fight. Pararescuemen, in contrast, are skilled in the use of all types of weapons and are prepared to fight their way into, and out of, highly dangerous situations to accomplish rescues. A writer on the SOFREP.com website points out, "They are not simply medics, and they are anything but unarmed. Their motto is *That Others May Live,* and their trauma medicine capabilities combined with SOF battlefield skills make them special even within the special operations community."

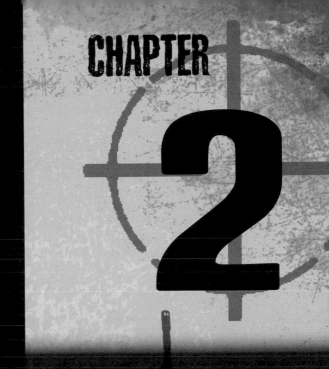

A CENTURY OF RESCUES

Rescuing warriors became possible only when aircraft were invented. The first rescue attempts were unofficial. No military unit existed for rescue of stranded warriors. But throughout the twentieth century, the U.S. military has learned from both successes and failures, and developed one of the world's best search and rescue (SAR) forces.

Airplanes first appeared during World War I (1914–1918). These rickety planes, made of painted fabric and lacking parachutes, quickly became a major force in the war. They could attack from above over the entire range of the battle area. The Allies sent forces of up to 1,500 planes against the Germans. But on-ground forces quickly developed ground-to-air gunnery to shoot them down. By the war's end, according to historians George Galdorisi and Tom Phillips in *Leave No Man Behind*, between 25,000 and

World War I airplanes were flimsy, crude, and dangerous. At first, they were used mostly for reconnaissance. One British general commented that airplanes were "useless for the purposes of war."

30,000 British, German, and French airmen had been killed. Pilots landing behind enemy lines were captured or killed. There was no way to rescue them. But several daring rescues did occur during World War I.

GALLIPOLI: THE FIRST RESCUE

In April 1915, the Allies invaded the Gallipoli Peninsula, in western Turkey, and began a months-long campaign. On November 19, squadron leader Richard Bell-Davies sent a full squadron to take out a rail junction where the Germans received supplies. Flight Sub-Lt. Gilbert Smylie's Farman bomber was shot and going down, but he unloaded his bombs over the junction and landed safely in a nearby marsh.

Smylie saw enemy troops approaching him. From the air, Bell-Davies saw them, too, and he was determined to rescue Smylie. Bell-Davies landed in his tiny single-seater Nieuport, narrowly missing Smylie's burning plane. Smylie removed his flying coat, climbed over Bell-Davies, and crammed himself into the small space behind the cockpit. He remained bent double, with his head touching the oil tank, during the forty-five-minute return flight. When the plane landed at base and the story spread, it sparked airmen's imaginations. They saw the possibilities for using aircraft to rescue downed comrades, and rescue would quickly become part of every air force.

PLANNING FOR RESCUE

After Gallipoli, people began to consider how to accomplish rescues. The most urgent need was for better aircraft. Between the world wars (1919–1939), airplanes were designed for passenger and cargo transport, as well as for the military. They became bigger and faster, and flew higher and farther. Amphibious aircraft made air-sea rescues possible. Eventually, helicopters were designed to do landings and takeoffs from very cramped locations on land— for example, small jungle clearings.

Germany was the first country to establish an air-sea rescue unit, shortly after Adolf Hitler came to power. Planning and training were done during

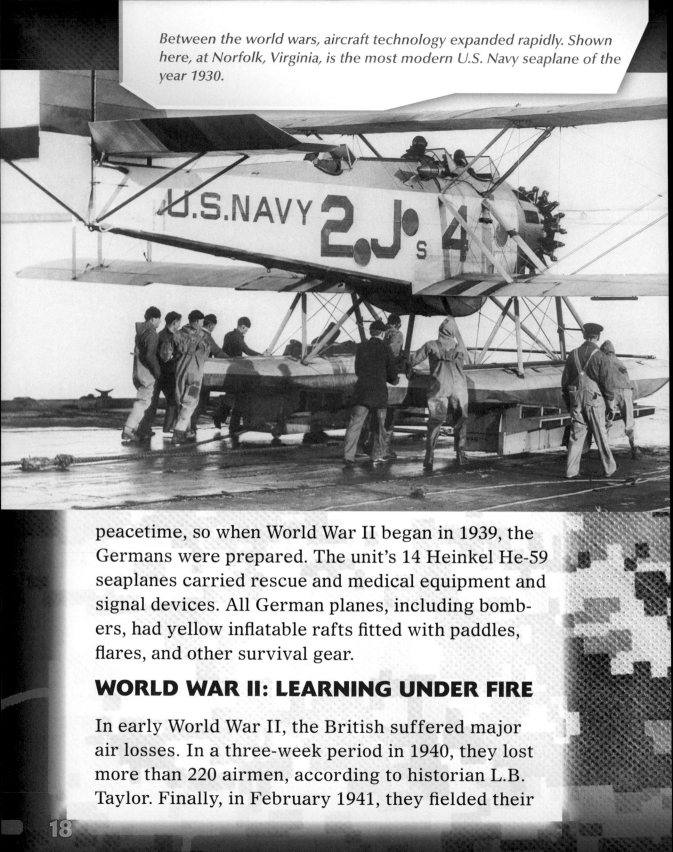

Between the world wars, aircraft technology expanded rapidly. Shown here, at Norfolk, Virginia, is the most modern U.S. Navy seaplane of the year 1930.

peacetime, so when World War II began in 1939, the Germans were prepared. The unit's 14 Heinkel He-59 seaplanes carried rescue and medical equipment and signal devices. All German planes, including bombers, had yellow inflatable rafts fitted with paddles, flares, and other survival gear.

WORLD WAR II: LEARNING UNDER FIRE

In early World War II, the British suffered major air losses. In a three-week period in 1940, they lost more than 220 airmen, according to historian L.B. Taylor. Finally, in February 1941, they fielded their own rescue squadron, borrowing ideas from the Germans. As soon as they launched the squadron and began to train aircrews to survive sea crashes, survival rates—and morale—immediately increased.

When the United States entered the war in 1941, it also lacked a rescue service. In Europe, Americans worked with the British, but in the vast Pacific waters, they were on their own. A few individuals worked tirelessly to improve the chances of pilots downed at sea. Major John H. Small Jr. wrote a jungle survival book and distributed it to Pacific aircrews. He also organized a small recovery unit consisting of four Catalinas (amphibious rescue planes). By April 1944, Taylor says, the Catalinas had saved 455 downed airmen.

TRIAL-AND-ERROR RESCUE

A dramatic Pacific rescue energized the formation of the first American rescue unit. Major-General Nathan Twining and fourteen companions crashed off Guadalcanal in the Pacific Ocean in January 1943. They had no radio and, although a full-scale rescue operation was mounted, they drifted for six days before rescue crews located them. Twining quickly became an advocate for a professional rescue service. The Air-Sea Rescue and Emergency Rescue School opened in spring 1944 at Keesler Field, Mississippi, and the first squadron graduated in July. Within six months, they had saved three hundred airmen.

Military leaders thought land-based pararescue was impossible until a daring rescue in August 1943. A C-46 transport plane developed engine trouble and crash-landed near the China-Burma border, carrying high-ranking U.S. and Chinese officials and famous war correspondent Eric Sevareid. There was no way to land a rescue plane in the mountainous jungle terrain. Dr. Don Flickinger, a surgeon and lieutenant colonel, and two medical corpsmen parachuted into the crash site, treated the victims, and (with the help of natives) eventually led them to safety. The military was convinced.

MAKING RESCUE OFFICIAL

To improve on the haphazard, trial-and-error rescues of World War II, military leaders needed a rescue unit that was a separate arm of the air force and that was well equipped, well trained, and combat-ready. The Air Rescue Service (ARS) officially began on March 13, 1946, at Andrews Field, Maryland. Six months after the first class graduated, according to Taylor, they had conducted sixty-four military and forty-three civilian aircraft searches and helped with other humanitarian rescues.

The Korean conflict (1950–1953) was the first major combat test for the ARS, and it proved the worth of helicopters and amphibious aircraft. According to author Tom Kaminski, the aircraft evacuated twenty-five thousand personnel, many of them soldiers behind enemy lines, who would have died if evacuated by jeep or truck. When the war ended, the forty-five pararescue teams returned to peacetime duties, most involving local air base rescues. Pararescuemen also began a new mission to support the U.S. "space race," rescuing astronauts whose space capsules landed in the ocean. In January 1966, the ARS became the Aerospace Rescue and Recovery Service, or ARRS.

VIETNAM

The young ARRS was unprepared for the challenge of Vietnam—a war spread across four countries covered in thick jungle growth. Rescue personnel had trained for Cold War rescues, not extreme environments and guerrilla warfare. They again learned by trial and error. Their helicopters (HH-43B and HH-43F Huskies) were not meant for combat. They were unarmed and small and had a limited range. Nevertheless, the HH-43 was used in more combat saves than the later CH-3 and HH-53 Jolly Green Giants put together.

The larger, faster CH-3s were modified several times, adding

On December 19, 1968, an HH-43 Pedro (Huskie) helicopter was used in the rescue of a downed airman from the jungles of Southeast Asia during the Vietnam War.

armor, defensive weapons, and air-refueling capabilities. The final CH-3E (called the Jolly Green Giant) held twenty-five fully equipped troops. The HH-53B Super Jolly Green Giant ("Super Jolly") was the first helicopter specifically designed for CSAR. It was larger, more powerful, and better able to hover and perform at high altitude. It had long-range fuel tanks, machine guns, and a rescue hoist with 250 feet (76 meters) of cable.

RECENT WARS

The ARRS served for eleven years in Vietnam, logging 2,780 combat saves, says Kaminski. The basics of a typical CSAR mission have changed little since then. Missions involve a search and rescue task force

A TYPICAL "JOLLY GREEN" RESCUE

Dave Richardson, a retired "Jolly Green" helicopter pilot, flew 107 combat rescue missions in Vietnam. He assisted in seven rescues that saved nine people. In a typical mission, Richardson says, two helicopters, a "high" and a "low," searched the dense jungle for the downed pilot. The low helicopter was the rescue craft; the high was the backup. Four prop-driven A1 fighters ("Sandys") protected the helicopters. Two flew ahead and two behind. When the downed pilot was located, the Sandys suppressed enemy fire while the pilot was hoisted to safety.

that varies with the mission. It may include fixed-wing aircraft, fighter planes, tankers, and an airborne command post, as well as rescue helicopters.

CSAR missions in Operation Desert Storm (the 1991 Gulf War) were limited because many aircraft went down deep inside Iraq where rescue was impossible. But rescue was now considered so important that, during the mid-1990s, several new CSAR squadrons were launched. In early 2002, when the U.S. invasion of Afghanistan was launched, air operations were delayed until a CSAR operating base was established. In the later Iraq invasion, military leaders divided the country into CSAR sectors with specific units assigned to each.

Lessons learned during wartime are incorporated into the next generation's pararescue training. Skills developed for rescues in extreme environments, such as deserts and jungles, are particularly valuable. CSAR units have been reorganized and moved under different commands, and training has become more intense, but PJs always remain ready to give their lives to save others.

DO YOU HAVE WHAT IT TAKES?

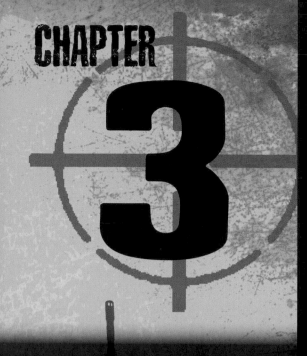

They are rousted from bed at 4:30 AM. They are on the go all day—running, swimming, calisthenics, weight lifting, obstacle courses, and classroom training. Every instructor pushes them to their limits. Finally, at 9:00 PM, they fall, exhausted, into their bunks. And, at 9:30 PM, a siren goes off, followed by an instructor shouting through a bullhorn. After half an hour's rest, they're up and at it again. They will spend another nineteen hours at the same breakneck pace, this time while sleep-deprived. This is "extended training day," or—as PJ recruits call it— "Hell Night." It is the recruit's introduction to the PJ development and indoctrination course (Indoc) at Lackland Air Force Base, Texas.

There are good reasons for this punishing introduction, according to pararescue instructor Staff Sgt.

Tim Hanks. PJs will undergo constant stress, including sleep deprivation, during real-life combat situations. A controlled training environment is the best place to learn how to handle it. It is also the best way to build teamwork, an essential PJ skill. "By the end of the night," Hanks says, "they will have realized they can't make it through by themselves." Teamwork (and stress) continues throughout the course. In one team-building skill, recruits carry a 450-pound (204 kg) iron railroad track during training. As one instructor put it, "The more you sweat in training, the less you bleed in combat."

INDOC

The Indoc motto, "Don't quit," follows recruits throughout the pipeline. Tech Sgt. Patrick Dunne, Air Force Reserve 920th PJ, oversees the P.A.S.T. (Physical Ability and Stamina Test) at Patrick Air Force Base, Florida. Dunne says that if you pass the P.A.S.T., you will likely get through Indoc. "I know what it takes to do this job," he says, "and I want the guys around me to be the best of the best. My life may depend on it." Other Special Forces operatives (Navy SEALs or Army Rangers, for example) become experts in one or two areas, but a PJ must excel in at least a dozen areas. Professionals this impressive cannot be mass-produced.

During Indoc, recruits do more than physical training. They complete weapons training and learn basic first aid, including cardiopulmonary resuscitation (CPR). They study leadership and pararescue history. They study the physics of diving, including dive tables and depth calculations.

THE PJ PIPELINE

Indoc begins the series of courses called the PJ Pipeline, which gives recruits the skills required to fight their way into an enemy area and locate, stabilize, and evacuate the wounded. After Indoc, recruits go to Florida for four weeks of dive training. They dive to 130 feet (40 m) and use SCUBA gear and closed-circuit diving equipment. This prepares them to infiltrate areas covertly and carry out underwater search and rescue

During Airborne School at Fort Benning, Georgia, trainees are dropped from a 250-foot (76 m) tower wearing a T-10 parachute. This is the standard parachute used for mass airdrops.

operations. In Fort Benning, Georgia, they undergo three weeks of U.S. Army Airborne training. Here they learn to do basic static-line parachute jumps.

The next stop is Basic Survival and Underwater Egress at Fairchild AFB in Washington. Here, recruits learn to survive in remote areas and extreme environments, including mountainous, arctic, and desert conditions. Underwater egress teaches them to escape a sinking aircraft. In the Military Freefall Parachutist School at Arizona's Yuma Proving Ground, they learn freefall, or HALO (high altitude, low opening), parachuting. In-air instruction focuses on controlling the body and maneuvering the parachute.

THE PARARESCUE TRAINING PIPELINE

Courses in the 2012 Pararescue Pipeline included:

Pararescue Development Course, Lackland AFB, Texas
(2 weeks)

Indoctrination Course, Lackland AFB, Texas
(9 weeks)

Combat Diver (Scuba School), Panama City, Florida
(4 weeks)

Basic Army Airborne School, Ft. Benning,
Georgia (3 weeks)

Basic Survival and Underwater Egress,
Fairchild AFB, Washington (17 days)

Military Freefall Parachutist (HALO), Yuma Proving Grounds,
Arizona (4 weeks)

PJ Medical (EMT-Paramedic Course), Kirtland AFB,
New Mexico, 28 weeks

Pararescue Apprentice Course, Kirtland AFF,
New Mexico, 24 weeks

Recruits then move to Kirtland AFB, New Mexico, for two final, intensive courses. After twenty-eight weeks of emergency medical technician (EMT) training, they receive certification through the National Registry as EMT-paramedics. Finally, they complete the twenty-four-week Pararescue Apprentice Course (Pararescue Recovery Specialist Course). Here, they test their combined skills in simulated field situations. They carry out medical care and patient evacuation. They practice field tactics, combat tactics, advanced parachuting skills, mountaineering, and helicopter insertion and extraction. After completing this course, recruits become PJs, or "Guardian Angels." They are ready, willing, and fully qualified to save a stranded, wounded person—warrior or not—from the harshest, most hostile environment. Combat rescue officers (CROs) complete the same pipeline as PJs, except that they skip EMT training.

HONING THEIR SKILLS

After completing the PJ Pipeline courses, PJs continue to train and test their skills. The air force sometimes sends PJs to private training schools in the United States to develop these skills to a higher level. At the annual two-week Angel Thunder exercise in Arizona and New Mexico, all types of Guardian Angels (PJs, CROs, and SERE specialists) work with other units of the army and air force, civilian and government agencies, and rescue forces from other countries. They also cooperate with regional hospitals and fire and police departments. During the exercise, participants complete simulated rescues. They train in weather and terrain similar to those in warfare situations.

PJs assigned to different rescue squadrons also train together, sharing their skills. PJs from Florida train with their counterparts based in Anchorage, Alaska. They practice cold weather combat skills and rescue skills, including night rescues and extracting "victims" from wreckage using ice tools. In turn, PJs from Portland, Oregon, train in Florida to practice water rescues. These cross-training exercises build teamwork while reinforcing PJ skills in different environments. To hone their paramedic skills, some PJs train with local emergency medical services. The Richmond (VA) Ambulance Authority (RAA) recently provided training for a group of PJs. While answering emergency calls, PJs responded to traumas similar to those in combat situations, including gunshot wounds and penetrating injuries.

Nine out of ten PJs "wash out" somewhere along the PJ Pipeline. But no one is ever kicked out—leaving is an individual's choice. PJs come through the PJ Pipeline as skilled, committed men, ready to save lives at all costs. According to Rob Lawrence, chief operation officer of Virginia's RAA, "They are very professional, yet humble, men, with an extreme mission focus who ultimately deliver good medicine in some very bad places."

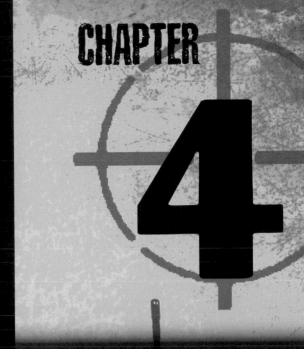

EQUIPPED FOR CSAR

Twenty-first century pararescue has come a long way from the Gallipoli pilot crouched in the back of a one-seater plane. Today's CSAR personnel are trained professionals, prepared for nearly anything, with the gear and technology to make it happen. PJs carry up to 170 pounds (77 kg) of gear when they jump to a rescue and use every kind of gear available. A helicopter pilot recalled a PJ saying, as they prepared to deploy to Iraq, "Sir, we need to bring our water gear." The pilot laughed because they were going to the desert. But the water gear went along and later helped rescue downed aircraft and Humvees from Iraqi lakes and canals.

THE CSAR TEAM: NOT JUST PJS

Personnel for GAWS, the Guardian Angel Weapon System, includes PJs, CROs, SERE specialists, pilots, and aircrew. The cockpit crew of the typical recovery aircraft, the HC-130 King, consists of a pilot, copilot, radio operator, navigator, and flight engineer. The cargo crew includes two loadmasters (responsible for cargo and parachute deployment) and three PJs. Rescue helicopters (usually HH-60G Pave Hawks) may be supported and preceded into the area by several types of aircraft. PJs sometimes enter on an HC-130 because the planes fly twice as fast as helicopters. PJs can parachute down, stabilize wounded personnel, and have them ready to evacuate when the helicopter arrives.

Senior Master Sgt. William Sine describes how a CSAR mission worked during a 2002 attempted rescue in Afghanistan. Sine led a PJ unit stationed in Jacobabad (or "Jbad"), Pakistan, about 300 miles (480 km) from Kandahar. When not on a rescue mission, HC-130 crews carried equipment, supplies, and personnel to Kandahar. On the night of February 16, after unloading supplies and leaving Kandahar, they were ordered to return and deploy for a rescue mission. A member of an Australian Special Air Service (SAS) team had hit a landmine and blown off a leg. They quickly returned, unloaded the HC-130's cargo bay, and prepared for a medevac (medical evacuation) operation.

The PJs jumped into the landing site carrying full equipment, including weapons and 80-pound (36 kg) medical rucksacks. The patient had lost a lot of blood, and the PJs gave him intravenous (IV) fluids. They wanted to insert an airway tube, but they feared that because he was semiconscious, they would make matters worse. They stabilized him as well as possible and transferred him to the helicopter that had just landed. Unfortunately, his heart stopped, and although PJs administered CPR all the way to base, he died.

Although the patient died during the rescue attempt, Master Sgt. Sine's mission report led to changes to the CSAR mission plan. After that mission, PJs were cleared to carry whole blood instead of just IV fluids. IV fluids restore blood volume, but they do not carry oxygen to the tissues, as whole blood does. PJs also began to learn a new airway technique. The technique, rapid sequence intubation, makes it easier to insert a tube and maintain an open airway.

THE WELL-DRESSED PJ

A PJ's standard gear includes:

- Body armor
- Magazines for weapons
- M4 assault rifle
- M9 sidearm (9 mm Baretta pistol)
- Radio
- Personal flotation device
- Standard MICH helmet with night-vision goggles (NVGs)
- Jaws of Life
- Medical pack

UNIFORMS AND GEAR

A PJ dropping into a rescue site wears a typical camouflage uniform and carries all the gear he might need. A radio keeps the PJ in constant contact with both his team and his aircraft. He wears the MICH (Modular Integrated Communications Helmet), which is lightweight, offers excellent protection from weapons fire, and works with most SOF tactical headsets and headphones. The Jaws of Life is a smaller, portable version of that used by fire departments and can cut injured personnel out of crashed aircraft. A PJ's medical kit is a portable operating room. It carries enough equipment to care for a multisystem trauma patient for seventy-two hours without being resupplied. This includes equipment for taking vital signs,

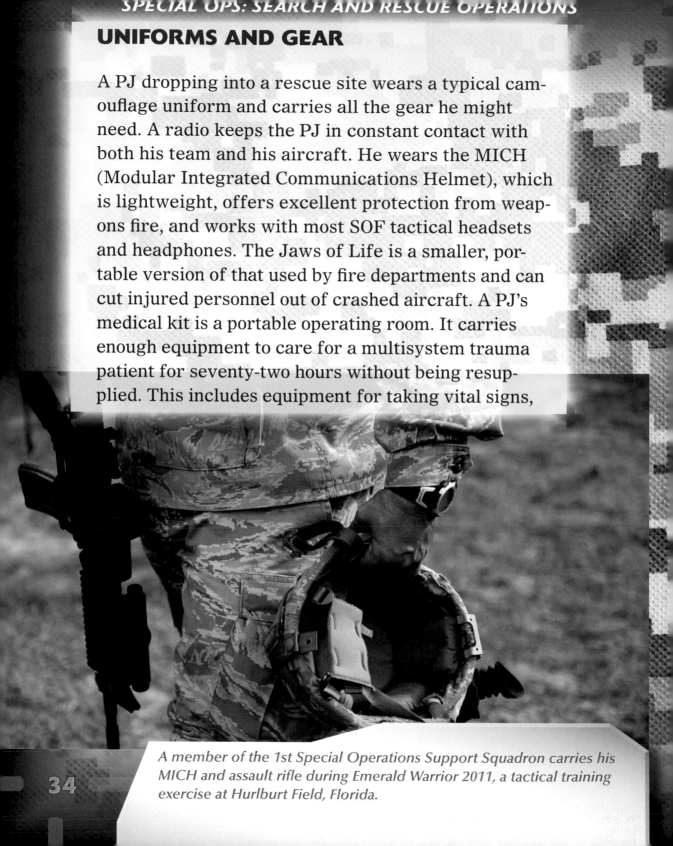

A member of the 1st Special Operations Support Squadron carries his MICH and assault rifle during Emerald Warrior 2011, a tactical training exercise at Hurlburt Field, Florida.

bandages, medications, surgical tools, needles and sutures, equipment to insert intravenous (IV) lines, splints, and more.

Other equipment is geared to the environment. Oxygen masks are required for high-altitude aircraft jumps and high-altitude rescues. Sea rescues use inflatable rafts, wet suits, scuba gear, and jet skis. Mountain and cold-weather rescues require special cold-weather clothing, snowmobiles, and mountain rappelling equipment. In relatively flat areas, four-wheelers and off-road motorcycles are used.

DROPPING IN: RESCUE BY PARACHUTE

Army airborne forces routinely do static-line parachute jumps to drop large numbers of troops into an area quickly. They jump from a low altitude (1,000 feet [305 m] or less). A "static line" attached to the aircraft opens the parachute automatically after approximately three seconds of freefall. This is the easiest form of parachuting, and all military personnel (including PJs) learn it first.

Special Forces, including PJs, more frequently use HALO/HAHO, or freefall, parachuting, to insert a few men into remote or dangerous areas. In HALO (high altitude, low opening) and HAHO (high altitude, high opening) parachuting, the jumper exits at a high altitude and pulls a ripcord to open the chute. HALO jumps are done in groups. Jumpers freefall until opening their chutes relatively near the ground. In HAHO jumps, the individual opens his chute at a high altitude, perhaps 25,000 feet (7,620 m), and glides cross-country to a landing site. The jumper maneuvers his chute to land at the assigned spot.

Military parachute rigs, or HAPPS (High Altitude Precision Parachute Systems), are also called stealth parachutes. They are designed not to be seen easily from the ground. They have attachment points where PJs can stow gear, plus a harness for oxygen equipment. They have special HALO altimeters to measure altitude and battery-powered lights for night jumps.

AIR SUPPORT FOR RESCUES

The HH-60G Pave Hawk helicopter is today's CSAR workhorse. It has a twin turbo-shaft engine and precision electronics, and it carries a crew of four. Each helicopter has satellite communications, color weather and infrared radar, flares, night-vision goggles, and a personnel-locating system. It also carries two 7.62 millimeter miniguns or .50 caliber machine guns and has an 8,000-pound (3,600 kg) cargo hook. It can lift a 600-pound (270 kg) load while hovering at 200 feet (60.7 m). The Pave Hawk can conduct day or night missions in the most hostile territory. It participates in all types of military and civilian rescues and evacuations.

The HC-130P/N King has been the USAF's only fixed-wing aircraft dedicated to personnel recovery for nearly fifty years. It underwent several upgrades and was the mainstay of CSAR operations

A U.S. Air Force HC-130P Hercules aircraft comes in for a landing at RAF Mildenhall, Suffolk, UK. This was the U.S. Air Force's only personnel recovery aircraft between 1964 and 2012.

in both Afghanistan and Iraq. It was responsible for equipment airdrops, getting personnel into and out of an area, and helicopter air-to-air refueling. The HC-130P/N usually flies at night, at low to medium altitudes, with blacked-out communications to avoid detection by radar and weapons. It is equipped with global positioning navigation, night-vision goggles and special lighting for night flying, flare dispensers, radar and missile-warning receivers, and high-level communication systems.

In 2012, the HC-130P was replaced by a new, updated model, the HC-130J Combat King II. The HC-130J still refuels helicopters, but it can also be refueled by a tanker plane. It has greatly improved sensors and is expected to be more reliable than the HC-130P—which is older than its pilots! According to Lt. Col. Christopher McCarthy, 563rd Rescue Group instructor pilot, "The J is light-years ahead of the P. It will make our job easier and make us much more efficient as rescue pilots."

MAKING SURE

When answering a distress call, CSAR must authenticate the source—that is, make sure the caller is who he claims to be. In war zones, the enemy might monitor or jam radio frequencies, or pretend to be a downed airman to lure rescuers to an ambush. So, when communication is established and before going in for the rescue, the CSAR unit asks for the downed individual's name, rank, and serial number as well as his physical condition. But they never give complete details over the radio—they use codes set up in advance.

CSAR troops are fearless and willing to enter any situation where someone needs rescue. But they also understand the dangers of the mission. So every PJ is grateful for each new piece of high-tech gear and equipment, and he immediately puts it to use to save lives—including his own.

RESCUING THE REST OF US

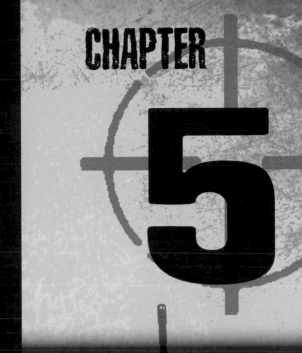

CSAR squadrons were formed for personnel recovery (PR) during combat situations. But in the last few years, their role has expanded. During the Afghanistan war, they were often requested for casualty evacuation (CasEvac) and humanitarian disaster relief missions. The air force is still the only service with a dedicated rescue force. While in Afghanistan, PJs regularly worked with army, marine, and British rescue forces.

A CHILLING RESCUE MISSION

In Afghanistan, PJs and army personnel conducted at least one humanitarian rescue inside a war zone. In 2010, a series of thirty-six avalanches occurred at an altitude of 11,000 feet (3,353 m) in Salang Pass. The 33rd ERQS Guardian Angel Team responded. This team, which usually performs water rescues in Florida, was stationed at Bagram Airfield, half an hour

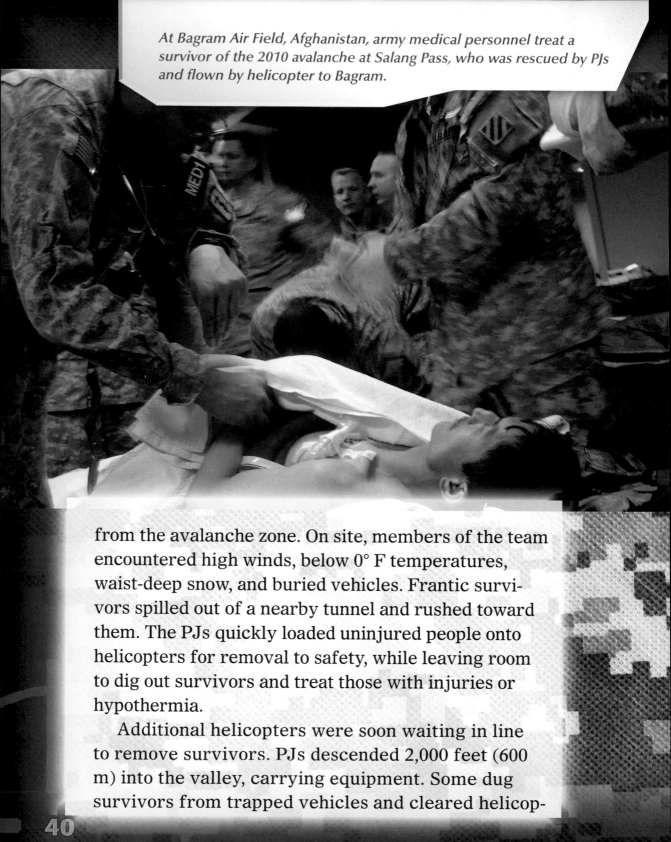

At Bagram Air Field, Afghanistan, army medical personnel treat a survivor of the 2010 avalanche at Salang Pass, who was rescued by PJs and flown by helicopter to Bagram.

from the avalanche zone. On site, members of the team encountered high winds, below 0° F temperatures, waist-deep snow, and buried vehicles. Frantic survivors spilled out of a nearby tunnel and rushed toward them. The PJs quickly loaded uninjured people onto helicopters for removal to safety, while leaving room to dig out survivors and treat those with injuries or hypothermia.

Additional helicopters were soon waiting in line to remove survivors. PJs descended 2,000 feet (600 m) into the valley, carrying equipment. Some dug survivors from trapped vehicles and cleared helicopter landing sites. Others treated the injured. Above, airmen watched for enemy activity, but fortunately, there was none. Over a seven-hour period, ten PJs, two airmen, and members of U.S. Army Task Force Gladius made twelve flights and rescued more than three hundred people.

CIVILIAN SAR

PJs are becoming increasingly essential in the civilian world, performing tireless work in response to natural disasters and terrorist attacks. Civilian search and rescue has its own law enforcement and civilian professionals. After natural or urban disasters, or while rescuing stranded individuals, everyone works together.

Civilian SAR training is done at the Coast Guard Training Center, Yorktown, Virginia, jointly operated by the U.S. Air Force and the U.S. Coast Guard. Since 1966, the center has trained twenty-nine thousand people from 148 countries in both maritime and inland SAR. Although they do not undergo combat training, trainees must be in excellent physical shape and have thorough knowledge of rescue procedures. A SAR team must deploy within thirty minutes of receiving a call from the National Distress and Response System (NDRS) and arrive at the rescue site within two hours.

The Federal Emergency Management System (FEMA) responds to urban disasters. They deal with floods, earthquakes, hurricanes, plane crashes, hazardous materials spills, and structural collapses. In 1991, FEMA established the National Response Plan, which currently sponsors twenty-five urban SAR (USAR) task forces, each having two thirty-one-person teams and four SAR dogs. After an urban disaster, FEMA teams support local and state teams.

USAR teams search for disaster victims and extract survivors from the wreckage. They ensure rescuer safety and provide medical assistance to the injured. In situations such as the 9/11 attacks, which involved building collapse, other experts are required. Heavy-rigging experts use bulldozers to move rubble. Structural engineering specialists determine the stability of fallen buildings. Hazardous materials specialists identify substances in the wreckage that might endanger survivors and workers. Finally, logistics specialists coordinate the activities of all rescue personnel.

SEARCH AND RESCUE DOGS

In 2010, the army's 911th Engineering Company, based in Fort Belvoir, Virginia, introduced the Urban Search and Rescue dog pilot program. The program was started because of the invaluable assistance provided by SAR dogs during the World Trade Center rescue effort. SAR dogs are trained to find a human scent and alert their human handler. According to author Julia Layton, superior smell, excellent hearing, and night vision enable a trained SAR dog to do the work of twenty to thirty humans. They can cover a search area much faster than a person can. They will scramble over and push through rubble or walk across unstable beams to locate trapped survivors. In wilderness situations,

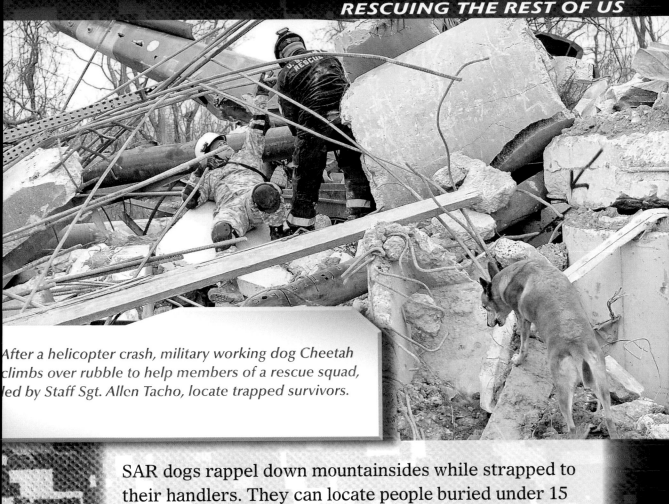

After a helicopter crash, military working dog Cheetah climbs over rubble to help members of a rescue squad, led by Staff Sgt. Allen Tacho, locate trapped survivors.

SAR dogs rappel down mountainsides while strapped to their handlers. They can locate people buried under 15 feet (5 m) of snow or bodies underwater.

THE TWIN TOWERS

On September 11, 2001, Al Qaeda terrorists hijacked four commercial jets. Two crashed into the World Trade Center in New York City, bringing down both buildings, and a third hit the Pentagon just outside Washington, D.C. The fourth crashed into a Pennsylvania field without striking its target. SAR crews from around the world responded for the rescue and recovery operations. According to Charles W. Bryant,

DOGS OF WAR

Military working dogs (K-9s) have been an important part of stealth missions in Afghanistan and Iraq. Military K-9s wear body armor and are trained to jump from an aircraft from 25,000 feet (7,620 m), strapped to their handlers. On the ground, they move ahead of their handlers, alerting them to mines, IEDs (improvised explosive devices), and human threats. SEAL Team K-9s wear tactical vests with speakers and night-vision cameras for communication with their handlers. Cairo, a Belgian Malinois, was part of SEAL Team 6, which located and killed Osama bin Laden. Another SEAL dog, Bart, and his handler, Master at Arms John Douangdara (also members of SEAL Team 6) were two of thirty service members killed in Afghanistan in August 2011, when their helicopter was shot down.

FEMA dispatched twenty USAR teams to New York to help with rescue and recovery—the largest USAR mission in U.S. history. In the largest deployment of SAR dogs in history, eighty dogs worked in twelve-hour shifts to sniff out survivors.

Chief Master Sgt. Paul Koester is one of many PJs who participated in the World Trade Center rescue and recovery. Koester qualified as a pararescueman in 1975 and later joined the New York Air National Guard as a reservist with the 102nd Rescue Squadron. In September 2001, Koester was on active duty on Long Island. When the towers fell, his squadron gathered their gear and flew by helicopter to the World Trade Center. For the next twenty-six hours, they helped remove survivors. His team rescued the last person found alive in the wreckage.

THE PENTAGON

Retired Staff Sgt. Christopher D. Braman was working as a mess cook in the Pentagon on September 11, 2001. After American Airlines Flight 77 slammed into the building, the scene was chaotic. People milled around in shock, and the area was filled with heated smoke. A former Army Ranger, Braman had served on the Combat Search and Rescue Team. His CSAR skills quickly took over, and he began to pull people from the wreckage. He went into the building again

Workers assess damage to a collapsed portion of Interstate 880 following the Loma Prieta earthquake in California on October 19, 1989. PJs crawled under the collapsed highway to rescue survivors.

and again, searching for survivors. He worked for three days straight, pulling sixty-four people from the wreckage. Only one of them, Sheila Moody, survived. Moody refers to Braman as her "Guardian Angel," a fitting tribute for a CSAR worker.

Wearing only a paint-dust mask, Braman had been breathing in a toxic mixture of jet fuel, asbestos, carbon monoxide, and human matter. He was treated for burned lungs and a respiratory condition doctors called chemical pneumonia. Braman still has nightmares about those days. He now speaks around the country, telling his story, and talking about patriotism and vigilance against future terrorism.

PJS FOLLOW DISASTERS

PJs go wherever disasters occur. In the 1989 Loma Prieta earthquake in Northern California, a highway collapsed and motorists were trapped in the wreckage. PJs were the only rescue personnel willing to crawl under the collapsed concrete to rescue survivors. In 2005, when Hurricane Katrina hit New Orleans, twenty Pave Hawk helicopters flew round-the-clock recovery missions for nearly a month. These PJ rescue teams moved more than three thousand people to safety. They dodged flying debris, downed trees, and power lines, and searched for victims in confined spaces. But they were happy to do it. According to Senior Airman Jack Earnshaw, of the 347th Expeditionary Rescue Group (ERG) from Nellis AFB, Nevada, "There's nothing more rewarding than giving back to our own country."

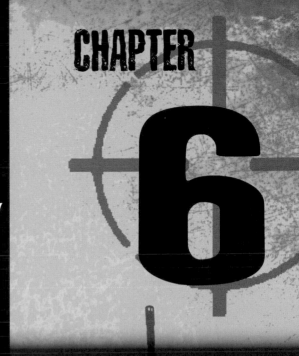

HEROES IN THE WAR ON TERRORISM

6

Every time the shout "Scramble, Scramble, Scramble!" rang out over Kandahar Airfield in Afghanistan, a rescue squad dashed for their helicopters and was airborne in less than fifteen minutes. This was the signal for a Category-A evacuation, indicating an urgent need for medical care and evacuation—a life-or-death situation. Less serious scrambles, or assists, also occurred regularly. Category-B indicates patients who are stable but need to be moved, and Category-C covers minor injuries, such as sprained ankles. Maintenance and operations personnel are as vital to the teams as PJs and flight crews. Helicopter maintenance crews spend more than fifty hours per week keeping the helicopters in top condition. A helicopter malfunction could literally mean the difference between life and death for PJs, crews, and patients.

Members of the 33rd Helicopter Maintenance Unit HH-60, from Kadena Air Base, Japan, perform postflight checks on a Pave Hawk helicopter during a search and rescue practice exercise.

Rescue squadrons were vital throughout the Afghanistan and Iraq wars (2002–2014). At Kandahar in 2010, the rescue squad included more than 160 troops from five different squadrons. About two-thirds of this crew's calls were to assist the Afghan army or Afghan nationals. Who they assist does not matter to PJs. Maj. Vic Pereira, 66th ERQS director of operations from Davis-Monthan, says, "We show the same dedication and duty when we pick up our Afghan allies as we would if we were picking up any of our coalition partners. We are proud to be able to show the Afghans that we care."

DECORATED HEROES

According to the air force, PJs have received the following decorations for bravery:

- 1 Medal of Honor
- 12 Air Force Crosses
- 105 Silver Stars

Airman First Class Bill Pitsenbarger received the Medal of Honor posthumously. He flew more than 250 rescue missions during the Vietnam War. When his helicopter was caught in enemy fire and withdrew, Pitsenbarger remained behind. He gave his life tending wounded members of Charlie Company, running ammunition between soldiers, and fighting alongside the survivors.

PJ SERVICE AND SACRIFICE

According to Jodi Kendall writing for the National Geographic website, PJs have conducted more than 35,000 combat and humanitarian rescue missions over the years. Since 9/11, they have carried out more than 12,000 combat rescue missions and more than 5,000 civilian rescue missions. In 2012 alone, they flew 4,500 Pave Hawk helicopter missions and saved 1,128 people—all with a total force of fewer than 500 men. Along the way, they have become the United States' most highly decorated enlisted force. According to John Stryker Meyer, writing for Sofrep.com,

Special Forces, including PJs, have suffered major casualties. Between 2001 and 2012, 270 Green Berets, 57 Navy SEALs, and 10 PJs were killed in action in Afghanistan and Iraq. Another veteran PJ, Chief Master Sgt. Nicholas L. McCaskill, was killed in April 2013, while working as a civilian security contractor in Afghanistan. One reason these wars had higher-than-usual PJ casualties was that insurgents began to target them specifically. They laid ambushes ("SAR traps") or placed bombs in areas where they knew CSAR teams would be.

INTO THE FUTURE

Any PJ will tell you: "A PJ is only as effective as his equipment." The Air Force Research Laboratory (AFRL) makes sure PJs go into the field with the most cutting-edge, effective equipment available. If what they need doesn't exist, AFRL personnel build it. Because PJs must be ready to respond instantly, the AFRL makes "rapid prototypes" of its new ideas. The Arachnipede Microbot is a microrobot designed to navigate confined spaces, collect data, and relay it back to PJs and medical staff. This new technology resulted in a prototype built with a 3-D printer. PJs test these prototypes in the field and provide feedback to the designers, speeding up the time from idea to final product.

The AFRL thinks of the PJ as a "mobile ambulance" who jumps to the rescue carrying 120 pounds (54 kg) of equipment. Decreasing weight and increasing mobility will improve the PJ's ability to do his job.

PJS ONSCREEN

PJ heroism has been dramatized in movies and on television. In 2013, National Geographic did a six-part series, *Inside Combat Rescue,* which chronicles a PJ unit's Afghanistan deployment. They placed tiny cameras on the PJs and in their helicopters to obtain detailed footage of actual combat missions. The 2001 movie *Black Hawk Down* describes a rescue mission to treat and evacuate Army Rangers during the Battle of Mogadishu, Somalia, in 1993. *The Perfect Storm* (2000), based on a nonfiction book by Sebastian Junger, describes an attempted rescue of fishing boats off the New England coast. The movie featured PJs from the 129th Rescue Squadron of the California Air National Guard.

Currently, the AFRL is developing a triangulating aerial robot to help PJs map a disaster site, narrow their search, and use cell phone signals to locate trapped individuals. Another need in search and rescue is speed. PJs often refer to the Golden Hour. That is, if a rescue team can arrive and provide medical care within one hour of an injury, the patient's odds of survival are dramatically improved. Any technological advance—such as the triangulating robot—that increases the speed of anyone on the team will help PJs meet this goal.

PJS NEVER QUIT: TEAM RUBICON

Since 2010, hundreds of retired PJs have joined Team Rubicon, a nonprofit volunteer organization dedicated

Members of Team Rubicon assist in recovery following a devastating F-5 tornado in Moore, Oklahoma, on June 2, 2013. PJ skills are vital in disaster relief as well as CSAR.

to providing disaster relief. These combat-seasoned PJs and other veterans realized that disaster conditions are very similar to those encountered during wartime: limited resources, unstable populations, and people caught in horrific situations. They also realized that a PJ's battle-tested skills could make a real difference—skills like emergency medicine, risk assessment, teamwork, and leadership. Team Rubicon is designed to "bridge the gap" (their motto) between natural disasters and conventional long-term responses. Teams specialize in rapid response, providing immediate relief until larger aid organizations are up and running. Their first mission brought medical aid and supplies to the residents of Port-au-Prince, Haiti, after the devastating earthquake of January 12, 2010. Since then, they have aided disaster victims in Chile, Burma, Pakistan, and Sudan, as well as in the states of Vermont, Maryland, Missouri, and Alabama.

Nick Jacobellis, writing for *Tactical Life* magazine, summed up both the value and the danger of a PJ's life: "It takes more than two years to train a PJ and less than a second for a Pararescueman to lose his life while performing his duties. Remember this the next time you hear that U.S. troops are being deployed in harm's way, because every time U.S. military personnel deploy for war, a contingent of U.S. Air Force PJs go along."

The air force describes a PJ's primary function as "a personnel recovery specialist, with emergency medical capabilities in humanitarian and combat environments." In other words, the pararescueman's job is to save lives. Every PJ takes this job very seriously. As one PJ put it, when describing why he chose pararescue over SEAL training, "I didn't want to kill people. I want to save them." This tiny force of dedicated rescuers is more important than ever, and whatever their mission, they hold steadfastly to their motto, "These things we do, that others may live."

GLOSSARY

AMPHIBIOUS AIRCRAFT Aircraft that can take off and land on either land or water; seaplanes.

CASEVAC Casualty evacuation; air transport of persons to a medical facility for initial treatment, on a transport having no designated medical personnel.

COMBAT RESCUE OFFICER (CRO, OR "CROW") An officer who is part of a pararescue team and who receives the same training as a PJ, except for medical training.

COMBAT SEARCH AND RESCUE (CSAR) Any operation involving location and removal of military personnel from hostile or dangerous combat situations, usually carried out by pararescue teams.

GUARDIAN ANGEL WEAPON SYSTEM (GAWS) Complete system required for a pararescue mission, including personnel, personal equipment, and aircraft.

HAHO JUMP A freefall parachute jump that is high-altitude, high-opening; the jumper opens the chute soon after jumping and glides horizontally to a landing spot.

HALO JUMP A freefall parachute jump that is high-altitude, low-opening; the jumper freefalls most of the way, pulling the ripcord near the ground.

MEDEVAC Medical evacuation; air transport of persons to a medical or surgical facility, with treatment of injured by licensed medical personnel en route.

PARARESCUE JUMPER (PARARESCUEMAN, PJ) A member of the elite U.S. Special Operations Forces; a "personnel recovery specialist, with emergency medical capabilities in humanitarian and combat environments."

PARARESCUE PIPELINE (PJ PIPELINE) Grueling series of courses, lasting almost two years, which a recruit must pass to become a pararescueman.

PHYSICAL ABILITY AND STAMINA TEST (P.A.S.T.) Intense physical exam that prospective PJs must pass.

SEARCH AND RESCUE (SAR) General term for the location and rescue of a civilian or soldier in a combat situation, disaster, or other dangerous scenario.

SERE SPECIALIST An expert in survival, evasion, resistance, and escape; part of a pararescue team.

SPECIAL OPERATIONS FORCES (SPECIAL OPS, SOF) An elite group of U.S. military forces, consisting of nine separate small groups trained in various military functions.

STATIC-LINE JUMP Parachute jump from a low altitude (less than 1,000 feet [300 m]), in which the parachute is attached to the aircraft (a static line) and is opened automatically.

UNITED STATES SPECIAL OPERATIONS COMMAND (USSOCOM) Military organization that directs all Special Operations Forces.

URBAN SEARCH AND RESCUE (USAR) Specifically targeting urban disasters, such as building collapses or earthquakes.

FOR MORE INFORMATION

Air Force Rescue Coordination Center (CONR-1AF)
1210 Beacon Beach Road, Suite 221
Tyndall AFB, FL 32403-5549
(850) 283-8080
Website: http://www.1af.acc.af.mil/units/afrcc
The AFRCC is the coordinator for United States
  inland search and rescue, coordinating activities
  in the forty-eight contiguous U.S. states, Mexico,
  and Canada.

Air Force Reserve Command
AFRC Public Affairs
255 Richard Ray Boulevard, Building 220
Robins Air Force Base, GA 31098-1815
(900) 257-1212 (recruiting)
Website: http://www.afrc.af.mil/index.asp
The official website of the Air Force Reserve Command
  includes news, photos, fact sheets, and information
  on reserve units by state and region.

Air Force Special Operations Command
100 Bartley Street
Hurlburt Field, FL 32544
(850) 884-2209
Website: http://www.afsoc.af.mil/library/afsocheritage/
  afsoccsarheritage.asp
The site outlines the history and heritage of CSAR professionals and includes links to other SOC websites.

Royal Canadian Air Force (RCAF)
442 Squadron COMOX
P.O. Box 1000, Stn Main
Lazo, BC V0R 2K0
Canada
(250) 339-8211
Website: http://www.rcaf-arc.forces.gc.ca/en/search
-rescue.page
This site describes the function of SAR techs and
their relation to the RCAF and civilian agencies. It
also provides a map of their locations.

**SARDUS (Search and Rescue Dogs of the United
States)**
46848 Highway 61
Otis, CO 80743
Website: http://www.sardogsus.org
This is the website of the national nonprofit organiza-
tion supporting search and rescue dog teams and
search managers.

WEBSITES

Because of the changing nature of Internet links, Rosen
Publishing has developed an online list of websites
related to the subject of this book. This site is updated
regularly. Please use this link to access this list:

http://www.rosenlinks.com/ISF/Sear

Bacon, Lance M., and Ronald L. Aiello. *Hero Dogs. Secret Mission and Selfless Service.* New York, NY: White Star Publishers, 2012.

Brehm, Jack, and Pete Nelson. *That Others May Live: The True Story of the PJs, the Real Life Heroes of the Perfect Storm.* New York, NY: Three Rivers Press, 2001.

Carney, Col. John T., and Benjamin Schemmer. *No Room for Error: The Story Behind the USAF Special Tactics Unit.* New York, NY: Presidio Press, 2003.

Harasymiw, Mark A. *Pararescuemen* (U.S. Special Forces). New York, NY: Gareth Stevens Publishing, 2012.

Harasymiw, Mark A. *Rangers* (U.S. Special Forces). New York, NY: Gareth Stevens Publishing, 2012.

Hirsh, Michael. *Pararescue. The True Story of an Incredible Rescue at Sea and the Heroes Who Pulled It Off.* Antenna Books, 2013. Amazon Digital Services, Inc. (Kindle Book).

Loria, Laura. *Marine Force Recon* (U.S. Special Forces). New York, NY: Gareth Stevens Publishing, 2012.

Masters, Nancy Robinson. *Pararescue Jumper* (Cool Military Careers). North Mankato, MN: Cherry Lake Publishing, 2013.

Nagle, Jeanne. *Delta Force* (U.S. Special Forces). New York, NY: Gareth Stevens Publishing, 2012.

Nardo, Don. *Special Operations: Search and Rescue* (Military Experience). Greensboro, NC: Morgan Reynolds Publishing, 2012.

Nelson, Drew. *Navy SEALs* (U.S. Special Forces). New York, NY: Gareth Stevens Publishing, 2012.

Peterson, Jesse. *Guardian Angel: Rescue on the Glacier.* Tuscon, AZ: Rescue Me Publishing, 2013.

Robbins, David L. *The Devil's Waters* (A USAF Pararescue Thriller). Seattle, WA: Thomas & Mercer, 2012.

Sandler, Michael. *Pararescuemen in Action* (Special Ops). New York, NY: Bearport Publishing Company, 2008.

Sine, William F. *Guardian Angel: Life and Death Adventures with Pararescue, the World's Most Powerful Commando Rescue Force.* Havertown, PA: Casemate Publishers, 2012.

U.S. Air Force. *Pararescue and Combat Rescue Officer Training.* Washington, DC: The BiblioGov Project, 2012.

BIBLIOGRAPHY

Air Force Special Operations Command. "Pararescue." PJ Training. Retrieved January 26, 2014 (http://www.afsoc.af.mil/specialtactics/pjtraining.asp).

Baseops.net. "Pararescue—Air Force Special Operations Command." 2012. Retrieved February 6, 2014 (http://www.baseops.net/basictraining/usaf_pararescue.html).

Department of the Air Force. "AFSC 1T2X1 Pararescue Specialty. Career Field Education and Training Plan." June 2002. Retrieved March 4, 2014 (http://www.pjsinnam.com/Downloads/Files/CFETP1T2X1.pdf).

Galdorisi, George, and Tom Phillips. *Leave No Man Behind. The Saga of Combat Search and Rescue.* Minneapolis, MN: Zenith Press, 2008.

Jacobellis, Nick. "Pararescue Jumpers." Tactical-Life, March 2009. Retrieved January 14, 2014 (http://www.tactical-life.com/magazines/tactical-weapons/pararescue-jumpers).

Kapinos, Tech Sgt. Joseph. "Squadron Highlights Capabilities During Afghan Rescue Mission." DVIDS (Defense Video and Distribution System). December 2009. Retrieved March 11, 2014 (http://www.dvidshub.net/news/42719/squadron-highlights-capabilities-during-afghan-rescue-mission#.Ux95cYVsvpg).

Kendall, Jodi. "Behind the Scenes with the Pararescuemen." National Geographic, 2013. Retrieved January 26, 2014 (http://channel.nationalgeographic

.com/channel/inside-combat-rescue/articles/behind
-the-scenes-with-the-pararescuemen).

Marion, Forrest L. *That Others May Live: USAF Air Rescue in Korea. The Korean War 50th Anniversary Commemorative Edition.* Air Force History and Museums Program, 2004. Retrieved March 4, 2014 (http://www.pjsinnam.com/Downloads/Files/1953%20That_Others_May_Live%20USAF%20in%20Korea.pdf).

Popular Military. "Join the Air Force > Pararescue Apprentice." Retrieved March 12, 2014 (http://www.popularmilitary.com/jobs/pararescue.htm).

Quade, Alex. "Elite Team Rescues Troops Behind Enemy Lines." CNN.com, March 19, 2007. Retrieved January 30, 2014 (http://www.cnn.com/2007/WORLD/meast/03/15/search.rescue/index.html?iref=mpstoryview).

Sine, William F. *Guardian Angel: Life and Death Adventures with Pararescue, the World's Most Powerful Commando Rescue Force.* Havertown, PA: Casemate Publishers, 2012.

Taylor, L.B., Jr. *That Others May Live: The Aerospace Rescue and Recovery Service.* New York, NY: Dutton, 1967.

INDEX

ABOUT THE AUTHOR

Carol Hand has a Ph.D. in zoology. She has taught college biology, written biology assessments for national assessment companies, written middle and high school science curricula for a national company, and authored approximately twenty books for middle school and high school students.

PHOTO CREDITS